31243 00 624 1912

Lake Forest Library
360 E. Deerpath
Lake Forest, IL 60045
847-234-0648
www.lakeforestlibrary.org

MAR - - 2021

D1031848

A long time ago, as a little girl,
I dreamed of traveling all over the world,
And often I'd ask about the past
Driving everyone crazy fast!

Amused by this my parents thought,
Why not call me "History" for short?

Since then I've traveled
By land, sea, and air ...

So read this book and
I'll take you somewhere!

Little Miss HISTORY Travels to
*Hyde Park, Home of*
*FRANKLIN D. ROOSEVELT*
*Presidential Library & Museum*
Volume 10

© 2019 Barbara Ann Mojica. All Rights Reserved.

Published in The UNITED STATES of AMERICA
by eugenus® STUDIOS, LLC
Books for All Ages
P.O. BOX 213
Valatie, NY 12184
E-Mail: Barbara@LittleMissHISTORY.com
WebSite: www.LittleMissHISTORY.com

ISBN-13: 978-0-9989154-5-6
Library of Congress Control Number:2019913684

IMPORTANT: Reproduction or distribution of this book, in any form,
is prohibited without written permission from the author.

Dedicated to
all the children
I have been fortunate enough
to teach.

# BARBARA ANN MOJICA'S

## Little Miss

# HISTORY ®

Travels to

Hyde Park, Home of
# FRANKLIN D. ROOSEVELT
Presidential Library & Museum

Illustrations by VICTOR RAMON MOJICA

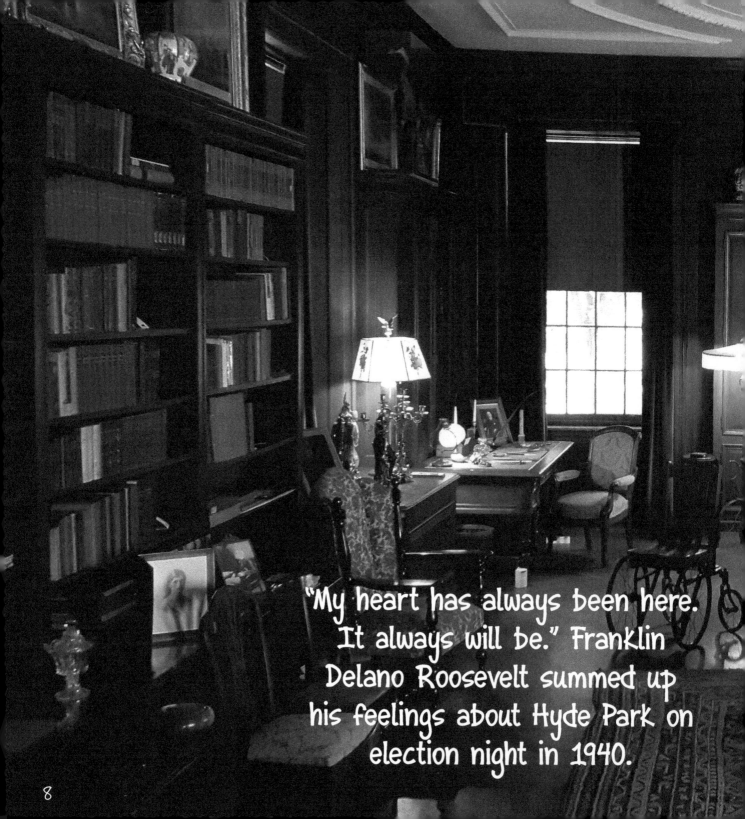

"My heart has always been here. It always will be." Franklin Delano Roosevelt summed up his feelings about Hyde Park on election night in 1940.

8

Franklin's father, James, purchased the home overlooking the Hudson River in 1867 for $40,000.

Franklin was born in this bedroom on January 30, 1882.

He married Eleanor
in 1905.

They had
six children.

FDR wanted to serve all the people.
Before becoming president, he worked as:
Assistant Secretary of the Navy, New York State
Senator, and New York State Governor

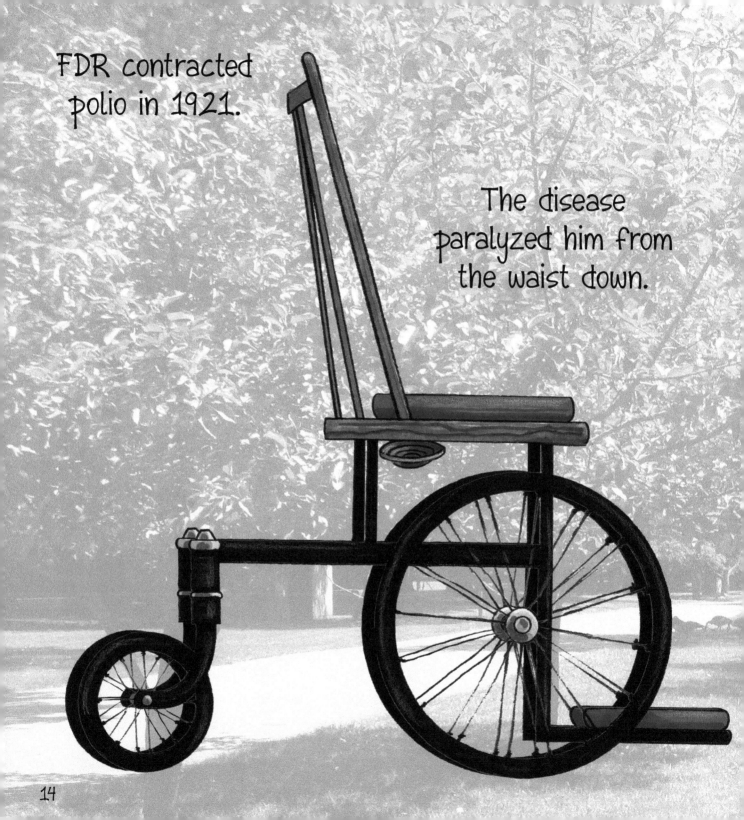

FDR contracted polio in 1921.

The disease paralyzed him from the waist down.

In 1932, Americans elected FDR to the first of four terms as president.

1932

1936

1940

1944

He was the only president to earn this honor.

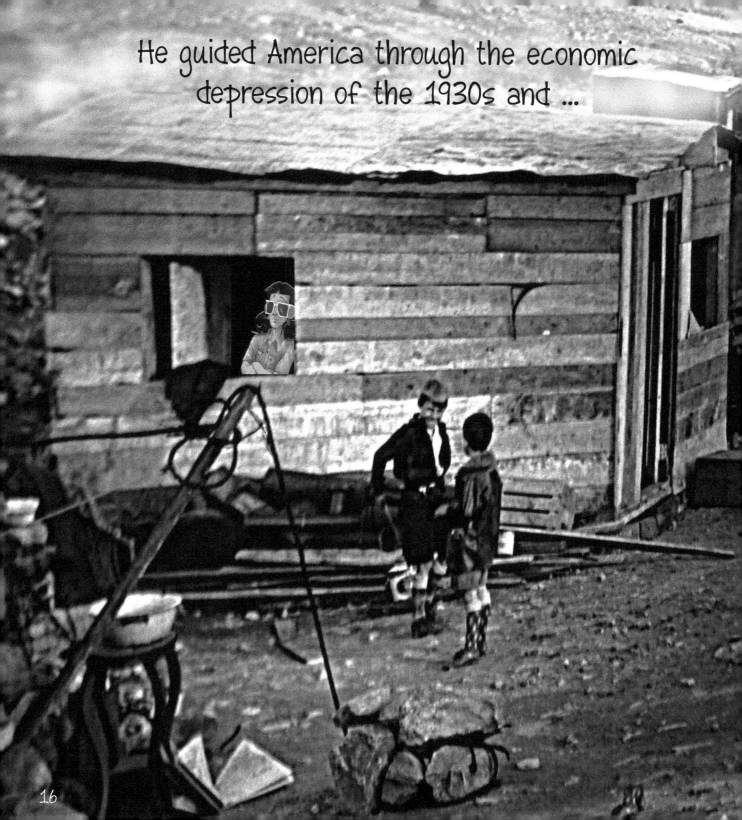

He guided America through the economic depression of the 1930s and ...

# ... World War II.

Franklin Delano Roosevelt redefined the role of government in the lives of United States citizens.

He set up the Civilian Conservation Corps which provided planting jobs for unemployed men.

His programs included Social Security to guarantee income for senior citizens.

He established the Federal Deposit Insurance Corporation to protect people if a bank failed.

Roosevelt set up the Securities and Exchange Commission to keep watch on the stock market.

FDR also instituted a minimum wage for workers and unemployment insurance.

President Roosevelt returned to Hyde Park over two hundred times. Some called it "The Summer White House."

Franklin loved trees and planted
more than half a million of them.

Historical cartoons about FDR's presidency greet visitors in the house's foyer.

23

A trunk elevator allowed the disabled president to get upstairs in his home at Hyde Park.

In the living room and library (see pages 8 and 9), Roosevelt worked on hobbies, like building model ships ...

... and his famous stamp collection.

The Roosevelts enlarged the house in 1915
to make room for their growing family.

Eleanor felt uncomfortable living in her mother-in-law's house, Sara, but she ...

... settled into this small room after FDR became paralyzed.

FDR slept in this "Boyhood Bedroom"
until he married Eleanor.

28

Each of his sons
later used it.

JAMES

ELLIOTT

FRANKLIN, JR.

JOHN

Sara, FDR's mother, used this room as her office, nicknamed the "Snuggery."

She ate breakfast here and managed the household staff.

Sir Winston Churchill, the Prime Minister of Great Britain, stayed in this room when visiting Hyde Park.

FDR used this bedroom as President. It was his favorite because of the view of the lawn and Hudson River.

There are stables a short walk from the house, where FDR spent much of his childhood.

FDR designed The Franklin Presidential Library
and Museum at Hyde Park in a Dutch colonial style.

The library opened in June 1941. It became the model for the nation's presidential library system.

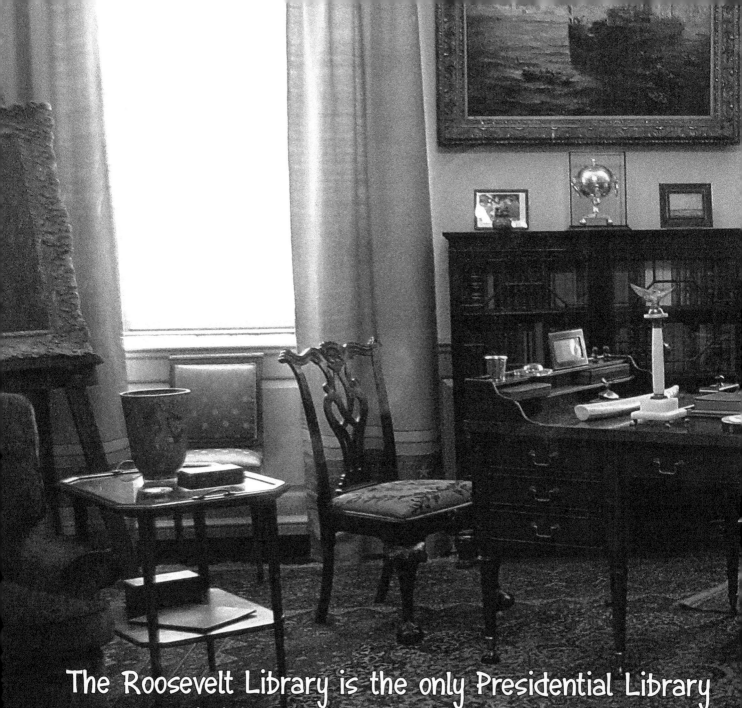

The Roosevelt Library is the only Presidential Library used by a sitting President. FDR conducted government business and received visitors here when at Hyde Park.

FDR delivered many of his "Fireside Chats"
to Americans from this office.

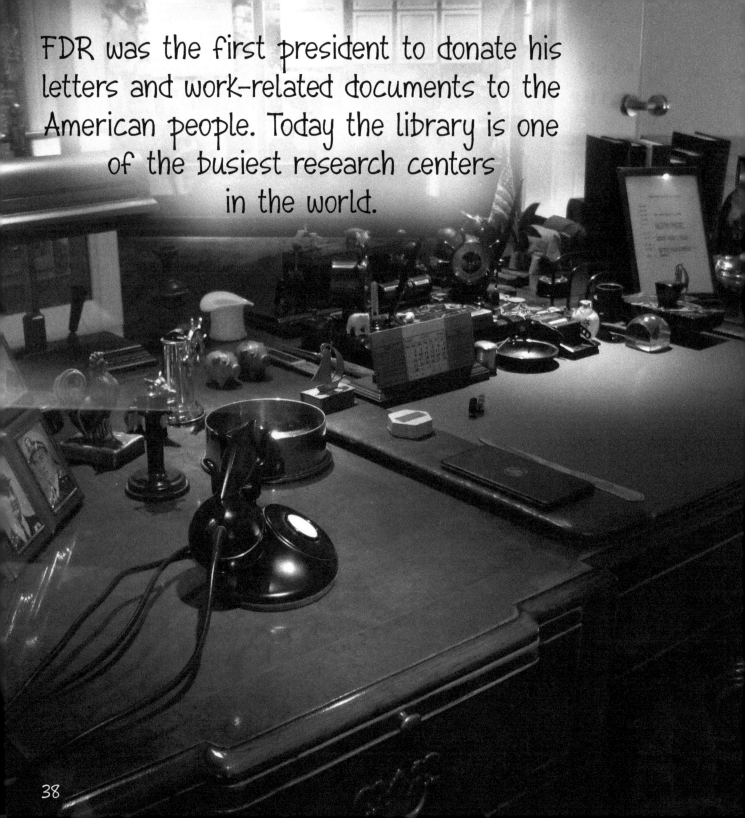

FDR was the first president to donate his letters and work-related documents to the American people. Today the library is one of the busiest research centers in the world.

This is the actual desk and chair
FDR used in the Oval Office,
and it's on display in the Museum.

As First Lady, Eleanor traveled and spoke
on behalf of the underprivileged ...

... and she served
as a delegate to
the United Nations.

COMMUNICA

RADIO AND TV
PERSONALITY

Eleanor Roosevelt's career as a radio and television personality started
during the 1920s when she began speaking about public issues on
New York radio stations. Later, as First Lady, she was interviewed on
countless radio shows, commenting on news events and public policy.
She also hosted several current events programs. In 1939, WNBC
called her the "First Lady of Radio." Though she donated her radio fees
to charity, ER endured criticism from some who felt this work was
inappropriate.

After the war, ER expanded her radio appearances. In 1948–1949 she
co-hosted The Eleanor and Anna Roosevelt Show...

Eleanor entertained family, friends, and heads of state at Val-Kill, her cottage at Hyde Park. She also ran a small factory business on the grounds.

FDR summed up his philosophy saying,
"The only limit to our realization of tomorrow
will be our doubts of today."

FRANKLIN DELANO
ROOSEVELT

# GLOSSARY

Civilian Conservation Corps (CCC) — gave young unmarried men jobs like fighting forest fires, digging ditches and planting trees

Federal Deposit Insurance Corporation (FDC) — provides insurance to depositors who put money in US banks

Fireside Chats — a series of 30 informal conversations delivered by FDR to the public on the radio

Foyer — an entry hall or open area in a house

Great Depression — the time period during the 1930s when many people were hungry, homeless, or out of work

New Deal — the name given to a group of programs during the 1930s set up by FDR to help the country during the Great Depression

Polio – (poliomyelitis) a disease caused by a virus that attacks the muscles and leaves victims paralyzed

Presidential Library – archive or museum that brings together in one place the documents and artifacts of a president

Redefine – to give something a new meaning

Securities and Exchange Commission (SEC) – an independent government agency that requires companies that sell stocks and bonds to provide full, complete and truthful information to investors

Social Security – a federal government program that provides income and health insurance to retired people, the poor, disabled and other groups

Trunk Elevator – an elevator powered by a hand crank

Underprivileged – people who do not enjoy the same standard of living or rights as the majority

Don't miss these other exciting adventures in the Little Miss HISTORY book series!

Next Stop...

O.K. CORRAL
GUNFIGHT SITE

TOMBSTONE ARIZONA

CPSIA information can be obtained
at www.ICGtesting.com
Printed in the USA
BVHW021821060121
596531BV00005B/9

9 780998 915456